Why Are They Like That?
Religious (or not)

Questions you've dared to ask, answered by real people, celebrities and experts

A book series based on the award-winning sharing project that's captured worldwide attention helping people in their personal, social and business relationships

Phillip J. Milano

For Robin, Jacob, Lucas and Ben

Publisher:
Y Forum
yforum@yforum.com

ISBN: 978-1-07-976376-8

Cover and interior layout by Sandy Weber,
Key 3 Creative, Jacksonville, Florida
Cover photo credit: Rawpixel. Stock photo for illustrative purposes
only; any person depicted is a posed model.

Content based in part on the popular Y? sharing project and Dare
to Ask column

Find out more about the author, upcoming books and speeches at
www.phillipmilano.com, www.facebook.com/PhillipJMilano or
@PhillipMilano.

Books In This Series

Why Are They Like That? Blacks

Why Are They Like That? Whites

Why Are They Like That? Hispanics

Why Are They Like That? Asians

Why Are They Like That? Gay Men

Why Are They Like That? Lesbians

Why Are They Like That? Women

Why Are They Like That? Men

Why Are They Like That? Rich and Poor

Why Are They Like That? Religious (or not)

Why Are They Like That? Disabled People

Why Are They Like That? Young and Old

Praise for the Y? sharing project and the book "I Can't Believe You Asked That!" (Perigee)

"Milano is quietly revolutionizing cross-cultural communication..."
- Pulitzer Prize-winning columnist Leonard Pitts

"If you've ever hesitated to ask a question because you think it might be considered insensitive or impolitic, now is your chance ... Nothing is considered out of bounds..."
- CNN Headline News

"(It) tells more about who we are and how we feel about each other than you're likely to learn from a dozen sociology texts..."
- Washington Post News Service

"Mr. Milano has dared to open the field of debate to the maximum..."
- Le Monde, Paris

"(A) remarkable contribution to cross-cultural understanding..."
- The (London) Guardian

"A truly rare achievement ... has the potential to have a profound impact on the way we all see and understand each other..."
- Playboy magazine

"It's an incredible book. It diffuses everything ... Nothing is off limits, and the questions have that childlike honesty to them..."
- Dee Snider, Twisted Sister; host, "Dee Snider Radio"

"A take-no-prisoners attitude prevails between the volume's covers . . . This book is hard to put down..."
- Midwest Book Review

"A+ (highest rating) ... Everything you wanted to know but were afraid to ask gets tackled here ..."
- Entertainment Weekly

CONTENTS

Introduction

Why Are They Like That? is a series of books based on an award-winning worldwide sharing project in which real people, experts and celebrities talk about things that make us different from each other. Silly things. Sad things. Funny things. Profound things.

Read with an open mind and we believe that by the time you're finished you'll have a much better understanding of how to make more and real friends, money and love. It's that simple.

Why? Because this isn't about trying to get ahead with diversity training. We are well beyond that. According to the Census Bureau, by 2050 the United States will have no racial or ethnic minority.

No, this is about moving past talking about how to understand each other to talking to each other. Right now.

That's why there's no agenda to these books other than getting the conversation going. We can discuss studies and methods for elevating social consciousness all we want, but there is no substitute for real dialogue.

That's where Why Are They Like That? stands apart from other books on the topic. You will see how people talk about their real differences of race, religion, sex, disability and more.

The success of the approach is proven: It's based on the ground-breaking Y? website project, blog and column that have attracted millions of visitors and worldwide media attention.

Our hope is that by reading, you will become more comfortable asking and answering the questions yourself, expecting the unexpected in return and helping change the ground rules for how we learn from and about each other. To that end, we wrap up each book in the series with our O.U.T.L.O.U.D. Method for Dialogue, with tips to help you get your own conversations started. Ultimately, that is what this effort is all about.

After all, if you want to make more friends, money and love, you better know the people you're talking to, selling to or opening to. Knowledge isn't just power. It's all power.

Enjoy.

Phillip J. Milano
Founder, Y?

Catholics getting crucified in the media

They asked:

So much is made of anti-Semitism and how ugly it is, yet anti-Catholicism is alive and well on TV and in the movies. Live talk shows seem obsessed to bash the church.

Rene, Port Orange

You said:

Catholicism is the largest denomination in the U.S. and world (more than a sixth of the planet's population), so what you may perceive as "a lot" is just proportionally appropriate.

Pete, 39, Pennsylvania

We found:

First, some housekeeping: At 1.2 billion, Catholics do make up more than a sixth of the world's population. However, there are more than 1.5 billion Muslims, and if being skeptical or hostile toward religion counts as a religion (they call it irreligion), those folks number anywhere from 800 million to 1.1 billion, according to Britannica.com, Adherents.com and other global surveyors of religious persuasion. (Keep in mind, pollsters count anyone who doesn't totally believe in somebody up there — even "Christian Atheists," who apparently don't buy into God but really like the moral teachings of Jesus.)

Let's start with Philip Jenkins, distinguished professor of history at Baylor University and professor emeritus of humanities at Penn State, who's written lots of books on religion, including "The New Anti-Catholicism."

He argues that in the case of abusive priests, the media tend to broad-brush the scandal as systemic.

"Even moderate commentators are writing as if priests around the world have taken secret vows of conspiracy, perversion, and omerta," he writes in The American Conservative. "Worse, this deviance is allegedly built into the church's structures of command and control."

But studies by the John Jay College of Criminal Justice in New York found that at most, about 4 percent of U.S. priests were accused of sexual misconduct with a minor between 1950 and 2002, and of those, 149 could be classified as "super-predators." Jenkins writes that he's not downplaying the situation, just adding perspective.

He adds in "The New Anti-Catholicism" that "In the media, Catholicism is regarded as a perfectly legitimate target, the butt of harsh satire in numerous films and television programs," while other faiths seem to get a pass.

He also writes that as liberal dissidents within the faith have blossomed, "For most of the media, a knee-jerk response holds that the Catholic Church and its hierarchy are always wrong, especially on matters of gender, sexuality, and morality."

Well, it sort of is wrong, at least when it tries to push its power and morality on millions of laity, said Ann Neumann (annneumann.com), editor of The Revealer, a publication of New York University's Center for Religion and Media.

"Nobody made up these sex abuse scandals. No one forced the U.S. bishops to say we will provide health care only in the way we want to — not providing contraceptives, not removing feeding tubes from vegetative patients, not offering tubal ligations or [embryonic] stem cell research ... About half their hospitals' money comes from federal and state funding ... but they refuse to operate according to individual rights."

And let's remember, the media thrives on controversy, she said.

"I'm afraid the media's job is to give readers something to read. I'm not sure it's their role to play something down," she said.

Is killing infidels OK with Muslims?

They asked:

Do most Muslims consider killing infidels acceptable or even expected?

C.D., Johnson City, Tenn.

You said:

No. Islamic principles forbid targeting civilians in war. To be honest, some people cheered on 9/11. But even they stopped when al-Qaida started targeting Muslims in Muslim countries.

Karim, 27, Muslim, Los Angeles

Some parts of the Quran are firmly opposed to this. Other parts say it is the right thing to do. Fundamentalists believe the latter.

Laurie, Jewish, Boston

The Quran is fairly mum on killing non-believers, although the folks targeted by the whacked-out fundamentalists — Christians and Jews — are mentioned as "Children of the Book" and are supposed to be respected as kindred monotheists.

A., 39, Animist female, Missouri

In the Quran there is plenty of backing to kill infidels or make them convert. Even in moderate sections it says you must tax exceedingly high on the infidel until they convert or die from poverty. Of course, in Leviticus [in the Bible] it says if a woman is not a virgin on her wedding night, she should be stoned to death. So I guess everyone picks and chooses.

Zechariah, Los Angeles

We found:

If you want to know how many Muslims think killing infidels is perfectly OK, you might want to see how many hold radical views in general. The book "Who Speaks for Islam?," based on a massive Gallup Poll of Muslims, tried to do just that.

It found, for example, that only 7 percent of Muslims felt the 9/11 attacks were completely justified.

When reminded that that amounted to 100 million Muslims worldwide, co-author Dalia Mogahed told U.S. News & World Report that most of those weren't terrorists but were part of the "cheering section" — and that 6 percent of Americans said they condoned purposely targeting civilians.

Muslim comic Ahmed Ahmed (ahmedahmed.com), who starred in the TBS comedy series "Sullivan & Son" and traveled the globe as part of The Axis of Evil Comedy Tour, the whole infidel issue is polarizing.

"The Quran is based on interpretation," he said. "And some people who interpret it are extremists."

Ahmed, whose "Just Like Us" documentary about comedians in the Middle East gained him an invitation to dinner at the White House with former President Barack Obama, said most Muslims don't force their beliefs on others, but do want to protect their religion.

The invasion of Iraq made the Muslim world fearful, he said, adding that the vast majority are peace-loving.

"I'm not plotting against Americans, nobody I know is," he said, laughing. "But hey, if I wanted to, I'd taint our ketchup supply, because America loves ketchup."

Ahmed did say he's pretty sick of all the suspicion.

"Like after 9/11, I'm at the airport and told the woman at the counter I'm a comic and I was running late ... she says 'Say something funny.' I said, 'OK, I just graduated from flight school.'

"She didn't laugh. The lady next to her, though, I heard her whisper, 'That was pretty fuckin' funny.' "

Blessed be: No grace or Sunday church for Germans?

They asked:

I notice many Germans don't pray before they eat, attend church or seem spiritual. Why is that?

Anjela, 30, Christian, Germany

You said:

In Europe, few go to church. It's the same in Australia. Most understand the church and its stories are wonderful interpretations from the past of why we exist. But they alone tell us little about our relations today.

Kent, 60, Episcopalian, Melbourne

Christianity to some of us is more than "stories." It is a creed, a code of ethics and beliefs.

Jack, 57, Christian, Suwanee, Ga.

In Germany, an active religious life with prayers, Bible classes and church attendance is a minority thing. You'll raise eyebrows if you pray in public, and would be considered immensely odd. Additionally, church attendance has been dwindling for decades, though people still pay their church taxes to support charity work done by church institutions.

T., 32, atheist female, Munich

We found:

While that secularist stuff does abound in Germany and Western Europe, wide swaths of folks remain religious. But in general, they don't air it out in public as much as Americans might, said Jutta Ittner, a Case Western Reserve University (Cleveland, Ohio) professor who teaches German literature and culture.

"Here there's a church on every corner," said Ittner, who is from Bavaria. "You can create your own church and find your own flock.

But in Germany, the priests and ministers are academics and belong to huge institutions ... so the masses don't feel personally attached. Here, religion seems a social thing, with lots of hugging and hand-holding. People in Germany would think they're in the wrong movie over there if they saw that."

Low church attendance and lack of a personal connection may also be because religion itself has been such a long institution in Germany — and suspicion of institutions heightened during and after World War II.

"The churches weren't beacons of truth in the Third Reich ... some wonderful religious people stood up against Hitler, but the church in general didn't," Ittner said. "Germans are very suspicious of any type of ideology."

Heap onto that requirements to pay church taxes and take religious coursework in school, and you get a populace that can harbor resentment toward religion.

"With the courses, you learn about issues, but not about a personal connection or about praying. [So you] don't get a feel for a real religious experience. That prevents an intimate understanding. And, you don't talk about it publicly. You'd be viewed as eccentric."

Some Jewish women are wigged out — for a reason

They asked:

I'm wondering why Orthodox Jewish women wear wigs.

Dwanny, 51, pagan, Fort Worth

You said:

When Orthodox Jewish women get married, they believe their real hair should be seen only by their husbands. It also has to do with modesty.

Dana, female, Minneapolis

Jewish women are instructed to "cover their beauty" so only their husbands may see. This is based on a similar passage that Muslim women interpret by wearing a head scarf.

Rosie, 16, agnostic, United Kingdom

All Orthodox Jewish women don't wear wigs, only the married ones. Or, they can wear a hat or scarf. It's because hair is considered a woman's crowning glory. So after she's married, she will only let her husband see her real hair. Strangely enough, wigs are now made so attractively that some Orthodox Jewish women wear gorgeous wigs over their own hair, which sort of defeats the purpose. But it's considered fine to do, as long as their own hair doesn't show.

Laurie, 55, Jewish, Boston

We found:

This one's roots are found in the Torah, and in a code of modesty in Judaism known as Tzniut.

Numbers 5:11-31 discusses how to find out whether a woman suspected of adultery (a sotah) has strayed.

This partly involves a priest uncovering or even "ruffling" her hair — the presumption being that a proper married woman should thus keep her hair covered, according to Orthodox Rabbi Yaakov Menken, director of Torah.org and author of "The Everything Torah Book" (Adams Media).

"It's about not being alluring to other men, and about maintaining the privacy of herself."

Many traditional Orthodox Jewish women wear a tichel (headscarf), snood (net-like headgear) or sheitel (wig).

And some of those sheitels, well, they're to die for. They can run into the thousands of dollars, according to Baruch Shlanger, an owner of Sheitel.com, a worldwide distributor of wigs (the "Sarah Palin Wig" only runs $795, though).

"Even if the wig looks nicer than her hair . . . well, there's no reason not to look beautiful after you're married. But hair is very personal, and it's required to conceal it," Shlanger said.

Menken concurs. The wig, no matter how pretty, is still fake and is easily spotted by Orthodox Jews, sending a clear signal the woman is married.

Because the wigs now look so much better, they are becoming more popular with Orthodox Jewish women, to the point the sheitel market is worth tens of millions of dollars a year in the U.S. alone.

"A woman covering her hair doesn't stick out as much today as in the past," Menken said.

All in all, it's not about repression of women, but avoiding a "buzz of distraction and sexual tension," he said.

"They are proud of what they have, but will not broadcast it. And remember, the men have to wear yarmulkes and dress in much less-varied ways than the women. We may get to choose our ties, but once we're married we don't even get to do that . . . and you can quote me on that!"

Hey kids, go exploring ... other religions?

They asked:

Do most Christians encourage their children to explore other religions?

Lauren, 18, atheist, San Antonio

You said:

From my experience as an ex-Catholic, no. It seems most religions . . . think they're right, and everyone else is wrong, and if you believe even parts of another religion, you're going to hell. A religion like that would not promote an open-minded approach to worldly religions.

Derrick, 19, Maple Grove, Minn.

It's important to have a basic understanding of other religions, but . . . we only are told to "explore" when our current religion does not seem right after much deep thinking about it.

George, Catholic, Jacksonville

True Christians know there is only one way to eternal life: belief in Jesus Christ as Lord and Savior. Because no other religion adheres to this teaching, true Christians not only do not encourage their children to "explore" other religions, we actively discourage it!

Melody, 43, Missouri

Since Christians believe that not believing in Jesus will lead you to hell, most Christian families would be horrified at the idea of their children looking at "those other" religions.

Dina M., Chicago

We found:

Studies do suggest that members of more strict denominations would be less likely to encourage their kids to go on a binge of religious exploration, according to Stephen Merino, research associate at the Association of Religion Data Archives at Pennsylvania State University.

As one might guess, people of more liberal faiths, for example Unitarian Universalists, would likely be more open to their kids learning about other religions because they value free expression, he said.

However, nothing in life is simple, now, is it?

Al Winseman, specialist in religion with The Gallup Organization, says what's most important to look at is how deeply committed one is to one's faith, regardless of denomination.

Surveys by Gallup have found that, generally, the more "engaged" people are in their faith, the less threatened they are by other religions, the more open they are to actively seeking to know about others' religious traditions, and more likely they are to feel respected by and respect those of other faiths.

For example, Gallup found in 2004 that among members who felt a strong sense of belonging in their congregations, 61 percent were "integrated" - wanting to know more about others' faiths. But among "actively disengaged" members, only 27 percent had an integrated view.

What's more, Gallup found that nearly 90 percent of Americans have a "live-and-let-live" stance toward those of other religions.

Misconceptions about who's tolerant and who's not often can be traced "to a difference between leaders' viewpoints and the person in the pew," Winseman said. "There's a gap there. Tolerance doesn't make the news. Intolerance does."

Spring line of turbans not likely

They asked:

You know how Islam people wear turbans? Do they ever make a fashion statement with them? Like do they have Louis Vuitton turbans, or turbans with checkered or plaid patterns?

Roland, 15, Clay County

You said:

Just a friendly note, it's not "Islam people," it's Muslim people or Muslims. Most Muslims don't wear turbans; turbans are traditional in some countries like Afghanistan, Sudan and Oman. They are virtually unknown elsewhere except among Shiia clergy. And the answer is yes, in countries where they are traditional, they come in all shapes and colors. Some are made of expensive materials and have brand visibility. If it is clearly a high-quality turban, it can be a class statement I guess.

Karim, 27, Muslim, Los Angeles

To follow up on the above response, "Islam" is the religion, like "Christianity" or "Buddhism."

Laurie, Boston

We found:

Now that Roland's up to speed on terminology:

There's some pretty heady, stylish Muslim and Arab garb out there (check out the hijabs, keffiyehs, kufis and veils at alhannah.com and artizara.com), but if we're talking turban, we're most likely talking about the headgear of Sikhs, most of whose 23 million adherents live in India but who can be found all over the world.

In fact, Sikhism is the only faith that requires wearing it as part of the actual religion, as opposed to it being a cultural norm, which is the case with most clothing in the Middle East, said Gurumustuk Singh Khalsa, founder of sikhnet.com. He also helps out with ratemyturban.com. (Haven't weighed in? We like manmeetsinghsaluja's powder-blue affair - chic and not overstated – but last we checked its rating was only 8.11 out of 10. Go vote.)

While designers like Ralph Lauren and Marc Jacobs have put out trendy $125 to $600 turbans of late, these are secular items for the wound-piece-of-cloth-deprived lady in your life and aren't associated with Sikhism.

Turbans for Sikhs do come in many different styles, patterns and colors, but they aren't as commercially "fashionized," Khalsa said.

"For a Sikh the turban is part of your identity, your body . . . It's about people recognizing who we are, so people know we are Sikh," he said. "But we don't do it as an ego thing, like 'Look how pimped out I am.'

"It's not about putting on a show, but if [a nice-looking turban] is within reason, that's OK. You just don't want to make a mockery of it, like branding it, which would degrade the purpose."

Incidentally, because of turbans' religious significance, the Transportation Security Administration recently changed its airport search guidelines so turbans don't have to be removed in public. Only if other methods like metal detectors, pat-downs or X-ray machines can't rule out a turban as a potential threat would a screener now be allowed to ask a passenger to remove the turban in a private screening area.

Should religious holidays be for everyone?

They asked:

Should all religions have specific days off school and work for their holy days or holidays?

Christy, 20, Tunkhannock, Penn.

You said:

It seems that would be fair. Why should some religions get their holidays off and not others? But we'd never get anything done if we did it that way. Some holy days are Saturday, others on Sunday, and even on Thursday. My holy days are full moons, dark moons and seasonal changes and cross-quarters. But many holy days don't need the whole day off. Sounds like a mess to me!

Jamie, 23, female, Bellingham, Wash.

This is supposed to be a country with freedom of religion, but it seems the only ones who get noticed are those who celebrate some sort of Christian religion. I feel we should acknowledge all or none.

Heather, 31, West Virginia

At my workplace, in addition to recognizing most federal holidays, we are given two personal holidays we can take at any time like vacation. In my case I can use them to attend Sabbat rituals that might have been difficult to attend otherwise.

Chris, Wiccan, Seattle

It would make sense, since we have Christmas off, but then there would be too many days off for all of the holidays, and the students' education might suffer.

Michael W., Chicago

We found:

What if you worshiped Al Seckel and John Edwards, creators of that fish-with-feet ichthys parody symbol that has the word

"Darwin" in the middle of it? You could put in for a day off to practice your non-belief belief.

And under Title VII of the Civil Rights Act of 1964, your employer may need to make a minimal, reasonable effort to accommodate your religious beliefs. The tricky part is trying to determine what "reasonable" is, said Charles Haynes, senior scholar for The First Amendment Center in Washington, D.C.

"An employer can say, 'Well this is going to cost me some money' or 'I can't find a replacement,' " he said. "Under current law, apparently that could be enough for the employer to not have to accommodate."

Some religious holidays like Christmas eventually became national holidays for secular reasons, because trying to run a business on a day when almost no one shows up for work wouldn't be practical. Now they're grandfathered in on the calendar.

Similarly, if a community has a huge Jewish population, its school district might shut down on Yom Kippur because the schools wouldn't be able to function with so many people staying home.

"A rule of thumb is that school officials should give students who are Christian, Muslim, etc., a reasonable number of excused absences for religious holidays, as long as the request doesn't interfere with the education of the child," Haynes said.

And as long as it's sincere.

"If a kid says 'I'm a Math Atheist' like they did in the 'Calvin and Hobbes' comic strip, that's not going to fly," he said.

Two faiths, four issues, six feet under

They asked:

I converted to Judaism 12 years back. My mother has decided to start practicing Catholicism again and announced to me, her only child, she wants a Catholic burial. I have issues with embalming, waiting past three days to bury, an open casket and a ceremony in a church. Please help! I want to honor my mother without dishonoring my faith.

It's Me, Jewish female, Dallas

You said:

Thousands of Jewish converts deal with life-cycle events of non-Jewish family. A rabbi can guide you.

Naomi, 54, Jewish female, Jacksonville

Your mother's funeral is ... about respecting her last wishes. Did it ever dawn on you that she may have had problems with your conversion to Judaism? Stop using your faith as an excuse to dishonor your mother, which is against one of the Ten Commandments, located in the Old Testament.

S.D., 38, Episcopalian female, Tampa

She should have a Catholic funeral. A funeral is ... a final assertion of what we believe. Nobody is telling you to worship Jesus, just be gracious. As for "dishonoring your faith," making a stink is not honoring your faith.

Jerry, 61, Jewish, Connecticut

We found:

Heed mom's wishes - though there may be some ways to feel better about it. So says Sue Bailey, who with Carmen Flowers authored "Grave Expectations: Planning The End Like There's No Tomorrow" about funeral and burial etiquette.

"Everyone has sensitive feelings," she said. "People who convert tend to be more strict ... and the mother also has gotten strong feelings about her own religion."

Bailey advised the daughter talk to her rabbi, but also offered these thoughts:

Have a Catholic ceremony, but quickly, perhaps with the body on dry ice so the casket can be open just a short time, and no embalming is needed before burial. Allow family to sit shiva -- a Jewish practice in which people stop by the house over a week's time with food and condolences. The body need not be present. Find a nice location outside a church for the Catholic service, if that's agreeable.

"In the end, though, it's about honoring the person, and the mom is not Jewish, so you kind of have to go along with what she wants. Think if the roles were switched and the mom said she couldn't carry out the daughter's wishes; she'd freak out."

Some things may have to just be tolerated, such as cremation, which does go against Jewish practice.

"Perhaps at least her organs can be donated and the ashes buried, so we can say you're saving another's life -- and God would always support that."

The final cut is too much for some Catholics

They asked:

If Catholicism doesn't allow sex without the possibility of conception, does that mean Catholic married couples can't have sex after a vasectomy, menopause, etc.?

Jim, Chicago

You said:

Most Catholics look at the teaching of sex for procreation only as a joke. For that matter, vasectomies aren't permitted under Catholic "law" because that's a form of birth control -- allowing sex without the possibility of pregnancy. To think millions of people quit having sex after the possibility of conception no longer exists is laughable.

Rachel, 36, Niagara-on-the-Lake, Ontario

The church accepts contraception as a side effect of certain medications used to treat other problems (birth control pills to control heavy periods or endometriosis) and recognizes the need for contraception in special situations such as medical problems. Even then, they ask that should conception occur, you be open to it. At least this is how the nun who did my premarital counseling explained it when I told her I needed to be on good contraception because should I conceive while on chemotherapy the baby would most likely have problems.

Susan, 37, Catholic, Chicago

A true Catholic man cannot have a vasectomy -- it's considered artificial birth control. Same story for female sterilization. Accepted Catholic birth control consists of abstinence (yeah, sure, in other words, having kids).

M. Maurer, 52, male, Poughkeepsie, N.Y.

We found:

First, vasectomies: not allowed by the Catholic Church.

"When we render the sex act sterile, we are saying we don't want to image the love of God," said Christopher West, a leading expert on Catholic sex teachings. "We want the pleasure but not the responsibility. As soon as you sever sexual pleasure from the possibility of procreation, any means of sexual pleasure can be justified."

So, do those with vasectomies have to remain celibate?

"If a believer truly repents for rendering the sex act sterile, the moral evil no longer exists," said West, author of "Good News About Sex and Marriage: Answers to Your Honest Questions About Catholic Teaching." "Also, vasectomies are reversible. If you can restore the physical evil of the vasectomy, you should."

Next, contraception in general: "In a sexual act, you must leave the possibility of human life entirely in the hands of God. With contraception, you are taking the power of God into your own hands," West said.

Finally, medical contraception: Intention is the key. According to the Catholic Church, the pill can be used for medical reasons but just not to avoid children. As far as a hysterectomy, getting one to remove a tumor would be OK because the main intent is not to sterilize the woman. (It's also for this reason that a married couple having sex after menopause is not immoral: It isn't the woman's intent to become sterile in that case, either.)

However, in the example of Susan above, using contraception during chemotherapy is not treating a medical condition per se but merely prohibiting conception, which would be immoral, West said.

The Jewish take on what happens after you die

They asked:

Do Jewish people believe in a life after death in heaven?

Dan, 49, Catholic, Mount Prospect, Ill.

You said:

Absolutely. After death, the soul goes to heaven or purgatory (no eternal damnation in Judaism).

Ed, 25, Jewish, New York

I feel considering an afterlife in your actions is wrong. For example, if I give food to a homeless person, I do it because God says I should give tzedakah (charity). If I did it because I was trying to assure my entrance to heaven, it would make my gesture seem selfish and less meaningful.

Thomas, 27, Jewish, Richmond, Va.

I've been told by a leading scholar of the Old Testament that the afterlife is an invention of Christianity. A very successful one, I might add!

Dan S., 66, Jewish, Boston

In general, Jews are much more interested in social justice -- their concept is of doing God's will to perfect the world.

Raymond, 68, Jewish, Portland, Conn.

Life, and living properly, is simply expected. It's not an optional thing, and no "reward" is a necessary enticement. By the same token, if one chooses to not live up to his or her obligations, no threat, no matter how dire (read: hell), would be a deterrent.

Rebecca, 25, Jewish, Miami

We found:

"Jews as individuals believe everything from absolute clarity that there's an afterlife to 'Are you crazy? When you're gone, it's over,'" said Rabbi Brad Hirschfield, vice president of CLAL-The National Jewish Center for Learning and Leadership in New York. "Jews, like all people, claim different parts of their traditions to help give them a sense of grounding and comfort."

An erroneous assumption is that Jews worry about this life while Christians worry about the next life, said Hirschfield, an Orthodox rabbi and co-author of Embracing Life & Facing Death: A Jewish Guide to Palliative Care (CLAL).

"It's irresponsible to say a Christian focus on the hereafter distracts from a commitment to making this world a better place, or to say that Jews focus only on the here and now, when we have plenty of literature that affirms that when it's over, it's not over."

The Talmud, in fact, discusses Olam Ha Ba (the World to Come), often referred to as the Garden of Eden, where body and soul reunite and one reaps what one has sown. Some interpretations say the more righteous receive a bigger share of the rewards.

"To simplify: Jewish life says focus on the here and now and the afterlife will take care of itself," Hirschfield said. "Christians say use the afterlife as a model and the here and now will be just fine. Both are beautiful ways to look at life."

But they're not very funny ways to look, now are they?

So, how about this:

In Jewish Literacy (William Morrow), Rabbi Joseph Telushkin notes that some Jewish folklore discusses a heaven in which Moses "sits and teaches Torah all day long."

"For the righteous people, this is heaven," he writes. "For the evil people, it is hell."

Does being gay "harm none" in pagans' view?

They asked:

Are pagans accepting of homosexuals?

Rebecca, 17, atheist bisexual, Jacksonville

You said:

I have a friend who is a lesbian and is accepted and very active among her pagan community.

Alaina, 28, Episcopalian lesbian, Cincinnati

Many Wiccans tend to be liberal in thought, while most Asatruar/Odinists tend to be much more conservative -- so Wiccans tend to be more accepting, while Odinists tend to view homosexuality as "anti-family." That has been my experience, and I am dating a woman who is a pagan, and all of her friends are pagans.

Tim, 39, straight, Jacksonville

Actually, many Asatru kindreds are very accepting of gays. When my friend Ryan (gay and Asatru) died, we had a special wake. Our steward and his wife were the only straight people there; all the rest were either gay or bi and were Asatru.

Danny, 45, Asatru, bisexual, South Korea

I tend to believe that generally pagans are more accepting of homosexuality than most other faiths, possibly because they themselves have been persecuted for their faith and understand what it means to be discriminated against and hated for who you are.

Shelly, 49, New Age bisexual, Pennsylvania

We found:

Pagans accepting gays? Sounds like downright Heathenry (the capital H variety, we mean).

Really, for the most part, pagans are welcoming of all types, said M. Macha NightMare, a San Francisco witch and author of "Pagan Pride: Honoring the Craft and Culture of Earth and Goddess."

"America is very diverse. We come together in interesting combinations. Most of our [pagan] working groups are very syncretic."

There's even the gay Witchcraft group The Minoan Brotherhood. It began in 1975 "as a response to the heterosexist culture of most forms of Traditional Witchcraft prevalent in the 1970s," which had held that the polarity of nature meant "magic must be performed between a man and a woman," according to www.minoan-brotherhood.org.

Some pagan groups are still uncomfortable with homosexuality, including some Norse-based ones, NightMare said (Asatru is also known as "Norse Heathenism," though she did not mention it by name).

"They feel there's a need for balance among males and females," she said.

But generally, a common pagan moral guide is "And it harm none, do what ye will," which basically means "do unto others."

"We tend to be open-minded," NightMare said.

Oh, and there's also a little thing called the Law of Threefold Return, she noted.

"What you put out in the world will return threefold. So you better be careful."

Islamic women and coming out from behind the curtain

They asked:

What is the purpose of the Islamic practice of Purdah (concealment)? I can understand the hijab, but I think imprisoning a woman in the house, deprivation of education and work and forcing her to wear those "body tents" are extreme.

Rebecca P., 14, white, Jacksonville

You said:

Most Muslim women cover themselves because they want to be noticed for their intelligence and knowledge, not their sexy curves.

HYO, 14, Muslim female, Detroit

Muslims cannot control their own government, thoughts, sexual urges -- not even their own oil wells without the help of the Western world. Controlling their women is their last shot at self-respect.

Tom S., 53, Christian, Manteca, Calif.

The Islamic world has problems and needs help solving them, but as long as the West takes this missionary, ignorant, holier-than-thou attitude, it's not part of the solution.

Karim, 25, Muslim male, Los Angeles

You have to question societies that object to a woman's right to cover herself but call nudity a "human right." Is a nun required to be "liberated" for choosing to observe the habit?

Nadeem K., 24, Muslim male, Manchester, U.K.

Women dying because they couldn't walk to a doctor? Or couldn't purchase food because their male relatives were off fighting a war? Choosing to wear a traditional outfit and being forced to die from neglect are two very different things.

Aysha, 27, Idaho Falls, Idaho

We found:

Koran 33:53 refers to the Prophet Muhammad's companions asking his wives to relay matters to him. Allah sent down the instruction: "And when you ask his wives for any thing, speak to them from behind a curtain, this is cleaner for your hearts and theirs."

On went the hijab for women and out came the general practice of "Purdah" in some parts of the world where Islam and Hinduism are prominent.

"Muhammad did provide for full participation of women, but after his death they became excluded," said Jane Smith, professor of Islamic Studies at Hartford Seminary and co-author of the upcoming Muslim Women in America (Oxford).

Cultural traditions of patriarchy arose, and males found it convenient to say Muhammad had affirmed exclusion of women, though the Koran verse referred only to his wives.

Women across the Islamic world are gaining more rights, but in some places women are literally still running for cover, Smith noted.

Henry Ford a poster boy for anti-Semitism?

They asked:

Is it true that Jewish people don't buy Fords?

O.S., Jacksonville

You said:

While most Jews would buy a Ford if that was the car they preferred, they are also aware that Henry Ford was a vicious anti-Semite. Many Jews will not buy a Volkswagen (Hitler's "People's Car"), although most Jews would not shy away from going to Disneyland, even though we know now that "Uncle Walt" was anti-Semitic.

Marianne, 54, Jewish, Portland, Ore.

Henry Ford was an outspoken anti-Semite. Still, I don't know any Jews who avoid buying Fords. Some avoid buying German cars because of the Holocaust, though.

Shirley, 50, Jewish, Missouri

I have never heard of this issue. The subject came up when I was a teenager in 1970, and my grandpa said he would not buy a German car. My dad said around that time that it did not matter to him. However, I would worry about some guy at work if he started quoting Henry Ford regarding the way the world worked.

Burt, 48, Jewish, Irvine, Calif.

We found:

You can still watch Mickey, Donald and the rest of the Disney bunch and feel OK. There's no evidence Walt was a virulent anti-Semite. However, early Disney cartoons contained some "unpleasant Jewish caricatures" (Disney's own Web site even admits it), as did toons from other studios of the day.

Henry Ford, though ... that guy had some serious anti-Semitic stuff going on.

In "The People's Tycoon," Steven Watts' 2005 bio, he outlines how Ford liked the nasty book "The Protocols of the Elders of Zion," which among other things claimed a Jewish cabal was trying to take over the world.

Ford owned The Dearborn Independent and in 1920 put forth a series titled "The International Jew: The World's Problem," which Watts wrote "examined a purported conspiracy launched by Jewish groups to capture social, cultural, and economic power and achieve domination around the world."

That light reading was just the beginning. More malicious articles followed, and after much public outcry, Ford finally apologized, though his sincerity was questioned. In 1938, he even accepted "The Order of the Grand Cross of the German Eagle," the highest honor given a foreigner by the Reich. Holy beyond-PR mess.

Thus, many Jews in the 1920s-1940s opted to stay away from Fords, said Aviva Astrinsky, head librarian at the YIVO Institute for Jewish Research in New York.

"It was an individual choice," she said. "Maybe some synagogues or organizations said to not buy Ford cars, but it was not an organized effort. Nobody can speak for all Jewish people."

Times changed, as they often do. By the '50s, a Ford subsidiary had opened a car assembly line in Israel, and the Ford Foundation now espouses multiculturalism.

"There's no prejudice against Ford now, it's water under the bridge. It's historical," Astrinsky said. "I'm Jewish and have friends who are Jewish who drive Fords."

He's burning to know about Godly punishment

They asked:

If God is better than us in every way, why does he have no moral problem sending billions of his children to burn in eternal pain?

Allen, 19, atheist, New York

You said:

God made us in His image to love and serve Him. He gave us free will to pursue Him or to pursue worldly gains. God wants us to choose Him but does not force Himself on us.

S.D., 38, Episcopalian female, Tampa

Someone with Judeo-Christian beliefs might say because He also gave us free will to sin or be righteous. Given that religion is a man-made construct, I would say this is simply one of the many inconsistencies. This is why it's difficult for rational people to believe in God, or hell or heaven, for that matter.

D., female, California

The Bible is very clear that He desires all to be saved. However, for those who don't believe or reject Him, they will go to hell. To reject God is to embrace the opposite: Satan. That means hell.

Paul, Appleton, Minn.

If God exists, he has all the faults of an average human. The Bible calls God a "jealous" God, proving that God is somewhat flawed. As for the question about hell, I guess he has no real problem sending people and unbaptized babies to hell.

Norbert, 17, atheist, Minnesota

We found:

The whole "God sending people to endless torture" nitpick often sends questioning people over the edge (to where is the debate).

Julie Ingersoll, associate professor of religious studies at the University of North Florida, said the question gained steam for Christians in the 19th century, and people have been wondering about it ever since.

"Some people now might feel that hell isn't a lake of fire, but is aloneness or meaninglessness ... that life on earth is made meaningful by God, and that hell is a life of no purpose."

Enough to set you spinning, right? Hopefully not on a rotisserie. A lot of this pondering falls in the category of theodicy, which looks at the problem of evil.

"It's usually framed as, 'If there's an all-powerful and all-loving God, how do we explain evil?' Some answer that God wants us to love him so much, but we have the freedom to choose, and this creates the opportunity for suffering," Ingersoll said.

God provides the guidance, according to traditional Protestantism, not the evil.

"Because of the fall of man, the teaching is that all humans deserve hell in eternity," Ingersoll said.

"So it's not 'How can God let there be hell,' it's 'How can this loving God rescue people from hell instead of giving them what they deserve.' "

But there's always that other, pesky view ...

"Atheists would say ... the concepts of heaven and hell keep people almost infantile in their ethics. Is it more sophisticated morally when a 2-year-old shares his toy because he recognizes others want to play with it, or because Mom's going to hit him if he doesn't?"

How do Catholics keep a lid on their family size?

They asked:

If Catholics don't believe in contraceptives, how do they keep from having a lot of kids?

Linzi, 17, Selinsgrove, Penn.

You said:

It's all about timing.

Betty, 30, Catholic, Jacksonville

The method taught at my church uses the woman's temperature to find out when she ovulates. I know when I'm fertile. That means that my husband and I abstain from sex every other week - one week because I am fertile, the other because I feel disgusting.

Cindy, 31, Catholic, Pittsburgh

Not every Catholic toes the line on what the Church says we should do. Different parishes will be more conservative or liberal. And it isn't like we have to send in surveys every year saying we do or don't use birth control. There are Catholics who use birth control, just like there are non-Catholics who do.

Melissa, 23, Catholic, Jacksonville

There are other methods that do not destroy a fertilized egg, but prevent one from forming. Just because the church teaches against contraceptives doesn't mean Catholics aren't using them.

Arnold, Christian, Edmonton, Canada

We found:

It wasn't long ago - like maybe nine months before May 29, 1962 - that some Catholic family counselors (at least one) were actually advising some of their parishioners (at least one couple) that they should enlarge their family. Some people who authored this book you are reading but prefer to remain anonymous owe their existence to these counselors, but that doesn't mean they have a biased, favorable, fist-pumping view of Catholics who enlarge their families.

The Catholic Church says artificial birth control is a no-no; it says to use Natural Family Planning, said Theresa Notare of the Natural Family Planning Program of the U.S. Conference of Catholic Bishops. This involves testing basal body temperature, cervical mucus changes and other neat or messy things to see when the woman is fertile.

The FDA says this is typically about 80 percent effective, though Notare said studies show effectiveness can reach 99 percent if couples train well and follow the rules religiously (OK, she said "closely").

"We have a theology of responsible parenthood . . . the Church has never said, 'Have as many kids as you can absolutely have,' " she said. "We say that sex is for bonding and for new life, but children have to be cared for and loved."

By the way, the average U.S. Catholic family is about the same size as the national average, around 2.6 people. In fact, 11 percent of Catholic families have three or more children, only slightly above the national average of 9 percent, according to the Pew Forum's 2007 U.S. Religious Landscape Survey. The fact that polls show about eight in 10 Catholics are OK with artificial birth control might have something to do with that.

Does mom need to be Jewish for you to be?

They asked:

Is it true that to be recognized as a Jew your mother has to be a Jew? And how come I only see white-skinned women who are Jews? Can only white people be Jewish?

Kofi, Episcopalian male, N.Y.

You said:

You only see white-skinned women who are Jews because you aren't looking hard enough.

Sarah, 35, New York

If you were to visit Israel, you would find the Falasha, who are from Ethiopia and are black-skinned Africans. Also, there are many Jews who are Persian, Arabic and even Chinese, Indian and Japanese. What you see are those Jews who are derived from Eastern Europe, who, of course, are white-skinned.

Sasha A., 25, Los Angeles

According to Jewish tradition, if your mother is a Jew, that makes you a Jew. (They went with that definition because there was no definite way of knowing who the father was.) Regarding whether only white people can be Jews: no. If your mom is a Jew, you're a Jew no matter what your color. And people of all colors, nationalities, religions, etc. are permitted to convert to Judaism.

Laurie B., 55, Jewish, Boston

There are different Jewish sects, and at least some of them accept converts. Some black guys who have converted are Sammy Davis Jr. and Rod Carew.

Cal, 47, agnostic, Lakewood, Calif.

We found:

We thought actor Adam Sandler would be great for this one, but were devastated to learn he got it wrong in The Chanukah Song with:

O.J. Simpson, not a Jew! But guess who is . . . Hall of Famer Rod Carew - he converted!

Apparently, while the baseball star had 3,053 career hits, a .328 lifetime batting average and a Jewish wife and kids, he never actually converted. (Sammy Davis Jr. did, though.)

So, sadly, it was on to the less-funny but more-informed Orthodox Rabbi Benjamin Blech, author of The Complete Idiot's Guide to Understanding Judaism and an assistant professor of Talmud at Yeshiva University in New York.

"Judaism is a religion, not a race, and it permits conversion to it, so anyone can become a Jew, no matter what color. I've had several students who were black, and one became a rabbi . . . the clincher is Moses, who was married to a woman who was black, Zipporah," he said.

But just so you know, conversion isn't a quick "git 'er done" type of thing. As Blech noted, there are books to be read, oral exams to be taken and, at the end of the process, bet din, where a Jewish court of three rabbis really grills you until it's satisfied you know the material, privileges and responsibilities of becoming Jewish.

On the other hand, if Mom's Jewish, you're automatically in, according to the Torah.

"It's a maternal link . . . the reasons might be that the mother is in the greatest position to influence the spirituality of the child - has the most power over what the child becomes," Blech said.

Do Southerners stick their noses into others' beliefs?

They asked:

When I moved to Georgia I was shocked at the presumption of my co-workers and neighbors questioning me about my religion. Why are Southern Christians so nosy? I also noticed a chill after revealing I wasn't interested in going to their church.

Mary, 42, agnostic, Atlanta

You said:

Welcome to the South! I have had many people try to get me to their church to be "saved." I have my own religious beliefs and understand what you mean when there is a chill. I have experienced this many times when I reveal I am Catholic.

Kris B., Knoxville, Tenn.

The Bible tells us we should tell others about Jesus in a gentle way.

Aimee, 51, Pentecostal, Jacksonville

It's an insult if you tell someone in the South you don't want to go to church with them. It makes it seem as though you dislike them . . . that they are not good enough to socialize with.

Shevronyouna, 20, Cleveland, Miss.

For the record, I don't think bad about any of you at all. The way you live your life is your business, and I don't look down on anyone who doesn't live their life like I do as a Christian, because no one is perfect.

Bradford, Tupelo, Miss.

Christians believe when a person dies he goes to heaven or hell. They don't want anyone to go to hell, so they are distressed when people don't want to talk about religious matters.

Rob, Jacksonville

Christianity plays a big role in the South. Asking you about your religion is part of being polite and welcoming. Someone who won't discuss their religion, therefore, is seen as rude and may be given the Southern version of the cold shoulder.

Shelly, 49, New Age, New Alexandria, Pa.

We found:

Don't think of it as Christians being nosy - think of it as you being honored, said the Rev. Jerry Vines, former president of the Southern Baptist Convention and retired pastor of First Baptist Church in Jacksonville.

"I think it's a great compliment to this individual [to be asked her faith] because it means her fellow worker who is Christian loves her enough to talk about spiritual things," said Vines, who now heads Jerry Vines Ministries (JerryVines.com).

That's no license to go all hard-sell on anybody, though.

"Christians should be as tasteful about the way they approach people as possible. I don't think people should be verbally abused and assailed on a constant basis."

OK . . . but what about the perception that Southerners really home-in on religion?

"In the South, we've perhaps heard the Gospel of Christ more than other parts of the country. I guess it gives them a bit of a fresher or more earnest approach."

That approach is all about learning whether a person knows about Christ.

"But, it's a gentler approach to [first] invite people to your church," Vines said. "Most Christians understand this is our great commission . . . to spread the Good News."

And yes, he did ask.

Learn your Bible history – in public school?

They asked:

The Bible was here before Christopher Columbus, before Lincoln and before Elvis. So why can't it be fashioned into a history textbook and offered as a course in grade schools?

Rhonda, 42, Christian, Knoxville, Tenn.

You said:

If we're going to go there, we need a book on Jews, the Buddha and . . . and . . . and . . .

Heather, 31, West Virginia

I do not think the Bible should be made into a textbook. However, I do believe there should be a Bible class in every school. Since our country was founded on a Christian basis, I feel everyone should be familiar with the Bible.

Mary, Jacksonville, Miss.

Hell no! All those people you mentioned are real people who lived real lives and left behind solid evidence.

Erika, 15, atheist, Allyn, Wash.

I think the Bible should be taught in school. There's a lot of great stories about morality in the Bible, which is something the American school system needs right now.

Hernando, Roanoke, Va.

In the words of George Carlin, "Keep thy religion to yourself."

T., male, Middletown, Conn.

Educators use more criteria for texts than whether or not the book predates Elvis Presley.

Rochelle, Williston, N.D.

We found:

And on the eighth day we did not debateth whether it be goodeth or evileth to teach the Bible in school, but instead approacheth the topic from a legal standpointeth. OKeth?

Charles C. Haynes, senior scholar at the First Amendment Center in Virginia who focuses on religion issues, wrote The Bible and Public Schools: A First Amendment Guide, a document that actually received the (legal) blessing of groups like the American Jewish Committee, Council on Islamic Education, National Association of Evangelicals and People for the American Way.

He recommends schools not "teach the Bible," but offer elective courses that teach about the Bible. If done right, and especially if other World Religion electives are offered, a school district can help protect itself against a lawsuit.

Problems arise when teachers aren't trained, he said.

"Few have a background in religious studies, and there is confusion . . . about the difference between teaching the Bible in Sunday School and teaching about the Bible in an academic setting."

One key to passing constitutional muster is for educators to use a textbook that guides students through the Bible with good scholarship and context.

Basically, he says, there's a middle ground between Biblical indoctrination and Biblical ignorance.

"You could say that about any religion: Should we not expose kids to what's . . . had a deep influence for better or worse in world history? Bible literacy is not about pushing religion, it's about giving kids an education they need in order to be part of this culture and world events."

Muslims, Jews and very scary pork?

They asked:

Why are Muslims and Jews so scared of pork? Do they think there is some disease in there?

S. Howard, 30, New York

You said:

We are not scared of pork! In the Torah, Moses instructs his people not to eat pork and shellfish unless it is vital for life (in the Nazi death camps we had to eat pork) because it is considered unclean. Ever seen the slop pigs eat? But many Jews (myself included) do not keep kosher because shellfish is so darn tasty!

Emily, Annandale, Va.

Touching pork for Muslims is closer to touching dung than something "clean" like beef or chicken.

Debora, 40, Muslim, Virginia Beach, Va.

The upside to all this, according to stories I've heard from a friend who grew up in Singapore, is that Muslim bullies would run in terror if he would come at them carrying pork.

Tomer, 32, Jewish, Eau Claire, Wis.

I don't think anyone is afraid of touching pork meat or pigs as though they have some disease or something. That's funny.

Noaf, 21, Muslim female, Qatar

We found:

Pork: The Other forbidden-in-Leviticus (11:7-8), cloven-hoofed, non-cud-chewing, rubbish-eating, doesn't-thrive-in-arid-climates, banned-in-the-Koran (2:173), filthy, more-liable-to-cause-diseases-such-as-trichinosis-if-not-fully-cooked White Meat.

Pretty much covers the past 3,500 years right there.

Rabbi Bob Alper, a popular stand-up comic, says some Jews feel the pig no-no is a divine thing, others a medical thing, and others an arbitrary thing meant to remind them that "every time you put something in your mouth you should remember that you're not just chowing down, but ... that every bite of food is a reminder of one's religious obligations as a Jew."

"It reminds me of a joke: A woman confessed that her family kept kosher at home, but not outside the house. She was told, 'That's good - your dishes will go to heaven.' "

Azhar Usman, one of America's top Muslim comedians (at one point he was writing a book titled Everything You Wanted to Know About Muslims But Were Afraid to Ask - No, Really Afraid), says one goal of Islamic halal dietary laws is to avoid impurity.

And no fair with the pork derivatives, either.

"For example, in Muslim parts of the world you can find certain candies you crave that are made with no gelatin. So we loaded up in Indonesia last summer. If I'd been stopped in customs on the way back, all they would have found in my bags was a ton of halal Skittles."

To avoid impurity, there's also a lot of washing up (wudu, or ablution) going on by Muslims before ritual worship.

"It's done by observant Muslims before prayers - even if you're at the office," Usman said. "The worst possible scenario is getting busted by your boss with your foot in the bathroom sink. How do you explain that? 'Excuse me, I'm just making wudu.' He'd be like 'You're doing voodoo?' "

No 'pane' a gain for Jehovah's Witnesses?

They asked:

Why do Jehovah's Witnesses churches have no windows?

Jimmy, 32, Catholic, Edinburg, Texas

You said:

Depending on the area, it may be safer to do without windows. I grew up in Chicago, and in the dangerous neighborhoods, the halls were either windowless or barred.

Lina, 20, Jehovah's Witness, Bradenton

Not having windows is also a cost-saving measure, as it is cheaper to heat and cool a building without windows.

Johnna, 27, Montgomery, Ala.

Rocks through the window can be a pretty expensive replacement.

Jim, 18, Grafton, W.Va.

I've heard it's so that they don't see the rest of the world burning during the Second Coming. Vandalism and lack of funds are a pretty weak answer.

Joe, Reno, Nev.

I have never seen a window in a Kingdom Hall. There is a more in-depth reason than vandalism. That explanation doesn't hold water. Their churches are not the only ones susceptible to that.

Joseph F., 42, Texas

We found:

Can people who live in glass-free houses throw stones?

Gaze out your portal and ponder that while we chat with ex-Jehovah's Witness Paul Blizard, now a Southern Baptist pastor in

West Virginia and prominent critic of his former faith, which he likens to a cult.

"They put no windows in because people have a tendency to look out the window rather than focus on the platform in front," he said. "It's just part of the mind control of The Watchtower [headquarters]: having members riveted toward the platform rather than having any distractions."

Not true, says J.R. Brown, national spokesman for Jehovah's Witnesses.

"Our halls vary with the climate and security concerns of a region. For example in the Caribbean they are open-air . . . but in the United States we have given quite a bit of attention to security and vandalism, so we will build halls without windows. And air-conditioning is expensive [with more windows]."

Headquarters in New York usually offers a half dozen designs to a congregation looking to build a hall because it's cost-effective, he added.

But . . . what . . . about . . . the . . . . mind . . . control?

"We do feel that if you are going to benefit from a session going. on, you should look at the speaker and focus on him. . . . Jesus said to pay attention to how you listen," Brown said. "But these are practical suggestions; as far as using a windowless structure to force that point of view, that's a figment of someone's imagination.

"We honestly feel we are not a cult. Our membership is based on people who voluntarily want to learn and dedicate their lives to God."

Kneeling, standing, sitting ... do Catholics know why?

They asked:

Why don't Catholics understand all the rituals they do and say?

Robin, Bastrop, Texas

You said:

Most likely the Catholics you've talked to didn't pay attention in Catechism class (yes, we have slackers). Or they only went to church to please their parents, and stopped at puberty - becoming part of the infamous "lapsed Catholics." I rarely go to church. However, I actually listened in class, and know why we do the things we do.

Sabie, 23, female, Greenville, S.C.

I have gone to Catholic school almost my whole life, and they never really get into the good stuff. I just have to learn that on my own. I suppose they do not teach it because they think it's over our heads.

George, 15, Catholic, Jacksonville

Catholic teachers never really have explained the rituals' meaning to us. Fortunately, the Mass is fairly self-explanatory, and people only need to sit through a few services to understand what's going on. The most important ritual is the Eucharist (bread and wine), which comes directly from the gospels. The confession ritual is a way to beg forgiveness and purify the heart. Most of the rest have come out of 2,000-odd years of history and serve to reinforce the community bonds so important to the Church.

Ange, 20, Catholic female, Australia

We found:

Bob Perron's 3-year-old daughter knew just what to do with her pew's kneeler during Mass: ride on that padded leather sucker like it was the pony she never had.

48

But she also taught Perron, a self-described "Catholic edu-tainer" who speaks to more than 60,000 youths a year nationwide about Catholicism, a valuable lesson about rituals.

During one service, a Eucharistic minister was placing unused consecrated hosts into a gold box near the altar, prompting Perron to tell his daughter, "Look, they're getting ready to put Jesus in the tabernacle."

She yelled: "They're going to put Jesus in a box? Don't worry Jesus, I'll get you out of there!"

The point, said Perron, whose Iowa-based "Stooge 4 Christ" Ministries uses humor as a teaching tool, wasn't that his daughter was being disrespectful, but that she had a relationship with Christ and believed he was real - a friend.

"We Catholics can sometimes miss the miracle . . . that Jesus is really present during the Eucharist. My daughter taught me the importance of having a childlike faith."

And while not all Catholics are up to speed on all rituals, Perron says surveys and his own work show that more and more Catholic youths yearn to discover these practices' origins and importance.

"Sometimes from the outside these rituals can kind of look funny, but . . . they express a deep sense of faith that has been passed from one generation to the next."

She's kvetching about her critical boss

They asked:

I work for an older, wealthy Jewish woman who walks into our office and begins by criticizing everything. I've been told this is typical of Jewish women. Is this a culture issue?

Thirty-Year-Old, St Louis

You said:

Jewish people have been persecuted and chased out of more countries than I have space to list. We have become survivalists. [Your boss] pays extreme attention to detail because as Jews we are used to our decisions having life-and-death consequences. If you aren't the best, you are dead or being sold a one-way ticket on a train bound for nowhere.

Rachel, 24, Jewish female, Oceanside, Calif.

I have worked with many a Jewish person, and they do tend to be aggressive, but as long as you know your stuff and do what you're supposed to do, everything works out.

Anabwi, 42, black female, Plantation

I don't agree it is a Jewish female trait to be critical. I have to say the Jewish culture tends to place a higher value on tolerance and respect for diversity than average.

Laura, Jewish female, Los Angeles

I am familiar with a Jewish-European mentality that thinks the maximally friendly attitude is to ... offer a positively critical review that improves a situation or person.

P.B., Jewish male, Davis, Calif.

Jewish mothers raise their daughters to perpetuate the notion that whatever they do is best. The Jewish momma dresses the best, cooks the best, observes rules the best and knows the answers to queries the greatest minds have not even thought of. What wondrous creation of humanity for a role model.

L.H., Jewish male, Fort Lauderdale

There is a Yiddish word for what this woman is doing: "kvetching."

Bakum, 28, Jewish guy, San Francisco

We found:

If your boss bugs you, be a mensch, get off your tuchas and talk to her! And don't tie her disagreeableness to being Jewish. It's a personality trait, not a cultural one.

That's the gist of advice from Barbara Held, a psychology professor at Bowdoin College in Maine and writer of Stop Smiling, Start Kvetching: A 5-Step Guide to Creative Complaining (St. Martin's Griffin).

"What difference does it make what the cause of the behavior is, anyway, if it disrupts the workplace?" she said.

Held, who is Jewish, distinguishes between kvetching -- complaining about life in general -- and putting down others. While the former can be a humorous stereotype of Jewish mothers (the masters of which might be dubbed "yentas"), the latter isn't typically ascribed to Jewish females.

"[Kvetching] is expressing the harshness of living: 'Oy vey, I have a bad cold! I'm never gonna get well. ... I'm never gonna finish this work,' etc.," she said. That's not a bad thing if it makes a person feel better and draws others to them.

Ultimately, even if data did link kvetching or criticizing to a certain culture, that wouldn't excuse behavior that creates problems, Held stressed.

Is flying the friendly racial-profiling skies OK?

They asked:

Is it so wrong to racially profile people who are flying?

Lisa, white, Custar, Ohio

You said:

I would be nervous if I saw a couple of Middle-Eastern people get on my plane. I think we [whites] should be aware of how the profiling makes others feel, but those who fit the profile should also understand that at the moment it might just be a necessary evil.

Jason, Kiel, Germany

I shouldn't be subject to racial profiling and harassment just to make xenophobic people like you feel safer.

KMW, 22, black/white male, Boston

[Oklahoma City bomber] Timothy McVeigh was a white male in his 20s, so, given the pro-profiling notion, all white males in their 20s should be considered a serious threat to national security.

Dee, Cleveland

People are always complaining about how easy we [Muslims] are getting it. Well, we aren't - we get harassed all the time. There . . . rejoice!

Karim, 27, Arab male, Los Angeles

We found:

What if conservative radio host Michael Smerconish, author of Flying Blind (which advocates racial profiling in airports), and Parvez Ahmed, former chairman of the Council on American-Islamic Relations (CAIR) and associate professor at the University of North Florida, got together for a nice chat on this?

Well, they didn't. But we did interview them separately, so maybe the banter would go something like this:

Ahmed: "The fear is very legitimate, but we must acknowledge it's a result of lack of knowledge. . . . The flying public should say something if they see something, but not if they see nothing."

Smerconish: "Profiling is absolutely necessary. The FBI says Al-Qaeda is reconstituting itself . . . and their surnames aren't Jones or Smerconish. There are still Arab extremists who threaten us. The common denominator of the 19 [Sept. 11] attackers remains constant."

Ahmed: "If someone is suspicious-looking, yes, pull them aside. But if you simply see a person with a different color, or a beard, that's diverting law enforcement from things of a genuine security concern. That's counterproductive."

Smerconish: "The blue-haired old lady out of Miami with a walker is undeserving of the same level of attention as Abdul flying in from Saudi Arabia. If that offends people, I'm sorry, but we need to use street-smarts and face the fact there are commonalities among those who threaten us."

Ahmed: "Smerconish and others are exploiting our fears. . . . Law enforcement agrees profiling is the wrong way to go based on race. It should be based on suspicious behavior. The process now is so haphazard. Yes, I feel the stares. . . . If a local agent can detain you for hours because he didn't like how you dressed that day, how have you been made safer?"

Smerconish: "Hey, when . . . bald suburban white guys like me start to threaten us, I'll change my tune."

Can't love convince atheists they're not alone?

They asked:

Why do atheists not believe in God? Do we need proof to believe in Him? Don't we only need love?

George, 15, Jacksonville

You said:

I am not willing to believe unless I see valid proof. My parents were scientists and taught me not to assume.

Lynn, 29, atheist, Washington, D.C.

If a person told you they had a friend they talked to all the time, but you never saw this friend, and they could not describe this friend or where this friend lived, wouldn't you think they were insane? Also, look at 9/11. Don't you think many people who were killed were praying to God? If there is a God, that God let them down.

Johanna, Stroudsburg, Pa.

Many atheists don't believe in God because they just don't want to be held accountable for anything. They refuse to accept that they may not have absolute control over their lives. After all, if no one is judging you, what's stopping you from doing anything you want?

Nanen, male, Memphis, Tenn.

We found:

Lots of ground to cover here. First, and most important, if there is a God, would he ever create a hot-looking atheist? Three words: Madalyn Murray O'Hair. But wait - an informal poll of the author's male colleagues at one point found that former American Atheists President Ellen Johnson, whose pic is all over the internet, rated a solid 8 out of 10. Now we're confused.

Can Johnson clear things up? Do you think we'd ask?

However, we did press her on the "God is love" thing.

"People will say, well, you can't see love, but we know it exists, so why can't God exist?" said Johnson. "Well, I can accept that . . . that God is an emotion, but not more than that."

The atheist can't disprove God, but asks for evidence from those who say there is a God, she said.

Penn Jillette, of the well-known atheistic magic duo Penn & Teller, had lots to say on this, too. But first, his rate-my-godless-face numbers from our female colleagues: Well, let's just say they showed no mercy on his non-soul, and leave it at that.

"Pretty much everyone is an atheist about every god except one," he said. "We atheists just happen to go one god more."

Regarding love, Jillette wondered why it can't satisfy people all by itself.

"To anyone who believes in God: Isn't love more than enough? The beauty of humanity, love for family, your favorite Jell-O . . . my love for my father and mother . . . why are you telling me that's not enough?

"People say 'I believe in God, and God is love.' OK, I say God is my Mini-Cooper. How can you have the hubris to say 'I feel in my heart there is a God, but I can't explain it.' "

And, contrary to popular belief, Jillette said, some surveys show that more atheists came out of the closet after 9/11, "because the idea that a belief in God by very pious people is a completely harmless thing went away for a lot of Americans that day."

The O.U.T.L.O.U.D.
Method to Dialogue

OPEN UP: This is mostly about opening up to yourself. Why do you want to engage someone? Is it for the right reasons? The answers might help you figure out how to approach another person. A friend once told me the real reason I started Y? wasn't for me to learn more about "Buddhists in Asia or lesbians in San Francisco," but because I wanted to learn something more about myself. He was right. Acknowledging that has helped give me perspective when considering others' answers.

USE YOUR HEAD: Plan for the right question. Not all questions need to be the "wet dogs" variety. Stereotypes and clichés don't work as well as sincere attempts to talk.

TIME IT RIGHT: Create the "O.U.T.L.O.U.D. Moment". Pick your spots for provocative dialogue. Find a genuine opening rather than create a false one. It's often during those down times between all the "vital" discourse that we can most easily find a direct path to someone's point of view. If you spend enough time sitting in the cubicle next to someone of a different culture, chances are there'll come a time — over food, perhaps, or during a power outage — when the topic you've been dying to broach will wend its way naturally into the discussion.

LOCK IN ON THE TARGET: Keeping things simple can give the best chance for getting another's trust and a meaningful reply. Some of the best questions at Y?, those that prompt the most telling answers, are also often the easiest to digest. Remember, it's not about winning your point. It's what comes from the heart that counts most — and captures people's interest. Talking from the heart also means easing into things by letting someone know *why* it would help you to learn the answer to your question before you ask it.

OWN UP TO ASSUMPTIONS: One of the most refreshing and repetitive surprises of the Y? project is the difficulty in predicting how a person will respond to a question. Blacks do not think in lockstep. Nor do whites. Nor Christians or Muslims. Nor gays or straights. Be receptive to another's ideas. Wipe the slate clean and listen to the content of the message, not the color or culture of the messenger.

UNLOAD YOUR EXPECTATIONS: Many of us are thinner-skinned than we'll admit. When we get hit with an answer or comment we hadn't anticipated, our emotions can often get caught off-balance, and our egos get bruised. The solution: Expect the unexpected. You'll never be blindsided or taken aback by information that doesn't gibe with your worldview.

DIGEST THE DIALOGUE: Learning about others doesn't stop when the talking's over. Assess what you're told and how it fits with or departs from your perspectives. Recap your discussion with a third party to distill the most relevant information into its most meaningful points.

ABOUT THE AUTHOR

Phillip J. Milano is the founder of Y? The National Forum on People's Differences, the acclaimed cross-cultural dialogue project that encourages people to ask unflinching, politically incorrect questions about our differences.

Since its creation in 1998, Phillip's web site, YForum.com, has attracted millions of visitors and thousands of questions and answers. He has been featured on CBS, CNN, BET and the BBC, and in numerous newspapers, including The Washington Post, New York Times and USA Today.

He is the author of the Perigee book "I Can't Believe You Asked That!" as well as writer of the pioneering newspaper column/blog "Dare to Ask."

Mr. Milano is a 25-year newspaper veteran. He received his Master of Business Administration from Northern Illinois University and his Bachelor of Science in Journalism from Southern Illinois University.

SPEECHES AND APPEARANCES

Mr. Milano is an in-demand speaker. For bookings, contact

Contemporary Issues Agency

809 Turnberry Drive, Waunakee, WI 53597-2256
Phone: 800-843-2179
Fax: 608-849-6311
www.CIAspeakers.com
Info@CIAspeakers.com